The Hebrew Workbook

THE
HEBREW
WORK
BOOK

WRITING EXERCISES FOR
BLOCK AND CURSIVE SCRIPT

WRITTEN BY MIIKO SHAFFIER

SHEFER

PUBLISHING

Written by: Miiko Shaffier

Illustrated and Designed by: Ken Parker (visual-variables.com)

Published by:
Shefer Publishing
www.SheferPublishing.com

For permissions, comments and ordering information write:
Miiko@LearnHebrew.tv

ISBN 978-0-9978675-5-8

Welcome

My name is Miiko. I live in Be'er Sheva, Israel with my husband Aaron and our nine kids.

In 2016 I started to teach Hebrew reading with a unique and super easy method. I put my method into book form that same year and called it **Learn to Read Hebrew in 6 Weeks!**

Learn to Read Hebrew in 6 Weeks! has taught thousands of people around the world to read Hebrew. I get emails almost daily asking me what's the next step towards Hebrew fluency.

This workbook is the next step! I'm proud to present a thorough and easy guide to Hebrew writing.

I'm so pleased to be with you on your Hebrew journey. Please be in touch! I love to hear from my students.

Miiko@LearnHebrew.tv

How to Use This Book

Hebrew has two styles of writing, 'block' and 'cursive'. Hebrew block writing is used like English print. It's used by children in first grade, in books and newspapers and on posters etc. Hebrew cursive is used like English cursive. It's used in handwriting and note taking.

In this workbook you will learn both block and cursive Hebrew writing.

There are two worksheets for each letter of the Alefbet. The first worksheet will teach you to write the Hebrew letter in block script. The second worksheet will teach you to write the Hebrew letter in cursive.

As you progress through the workbook you'll find worksheets to practice words and sentences that can be written with only the letters and vowels you've learned to write up until that point. These worksheets cover both block and cursive writing, and include the translations and transliterations of the words.

There are worksheets to practice writing the Hebrew vowels. Hebrew vowels look the same in both block and cursive.

The last section of the workbook includes some common phrases and some basic vocabulary words. These worksheets cover both block and cursive writing and also have translations and transliterations.

If you prefer to learn cursive writing only after you've fully completed learning block script, you can skip the cursive sections the first time you work through the workbook. Once you completeall the block worksheets just go back to the beginning of the book and work through the cursive worksheets.

In my book *Learn to Read Hebrew in 6 Weeks!* I use cute pictures to remind my students of the sound each Hebrew letter makes. I've included these fun and helpful reminders in this workbook. As you learn to write, these pictures reinforce reading skills even for those who didn't learn to read Hebrew using my method.

Handy Tip

Here's a practical and useful tip to make the most of The Hebrew Writing Workbook. Cut the practice pages out of the workbook as close to the binding as you can. Put all the practice pages in clear plastic sheet protectors in a three ring binder. Use a fine-tip dry erase marker to trace the letters and practice your writing. This way you can re-use each practice page as many times as you like.

Transliteration

I use the system of transliteration that I created for my book *Learn to Read Hebrew in 6 Weeks*. It's designed to have the reader pronouncing the Hebrew words accurately without ever having heard a Hebrew speaker pronounce those words.

Each consonant is represented as a capital letter and each vowel by small letters.

The silent letters Aleph (א) and Ayin (ע) are represented by an apostrophe (')

The silent vowel 'Shva' (:) is represented as a hyphen (-).

This system removes any ambiguity in how exactly to pronounce each word.

For example let's look at the first word in the Hebrew Scripture.

We transliterate it:

B-Reh'SHeeYT

Others may transliterate it Bereshit or Bresheet but then you wouldn't know if the vowels are long or short.

Note:

The CH does not represent the ch sound like in *chair* or *chest*. In fact, Hebrew doesn't have the ch sound like *chair* or *chest* at all.

The CH represents the letters CHehT(ח) and CHahF(כ) and Final ChahF(ך). These letters make a sound not found in the English language. It's a chokey sound that almost sounds like a kitten purring but much harsher. Think about the ch in the name of the composer Bach.

If you learned to read Hebrew using my other book, you are already well familiar with my system of transliteration. But in case you learned to read Hebrew elsewhere, here's a key to make sure
it's clear.

NOW
LET'S GET
STARTED!

THE LETTER " 'ahLehF "

The letter 'ahLehF is silent.
It's all arms and legs, but
has no voice.

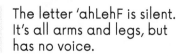

" 'ahLehF " CURSIVE

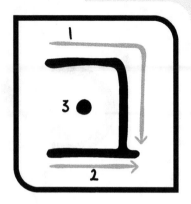

THE LETTER **"BehT"**

The letter BehT looks like a ball in a box. It makes the sound of the English letter "B".

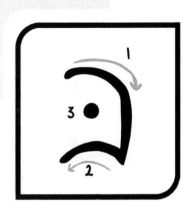

"**BehT**" CURSIVE

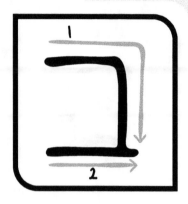

THE LETTER "VehT"

The letter VehT has a Vacant Void where the ball should be. It makes the sound of the English letter "V".

VACANT!

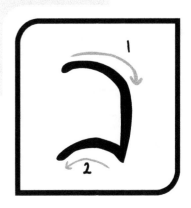

"**VehT**" CURSIVE

THE "PahTahCH" VOWEL

The PahTahCH makes the sound of the English letter combination "ah" or the "a" in far. The PahTahCH hangs below the line.

Write **PahTahCH** below the letters

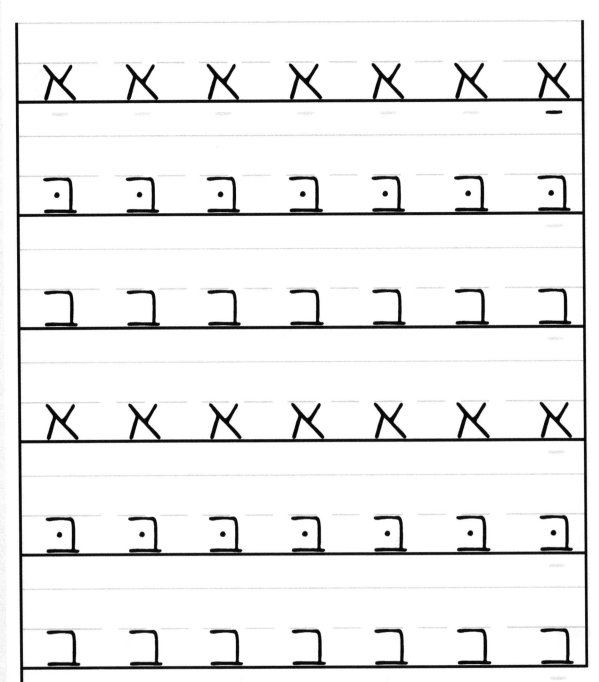

THE "KahMahTZ" VOWEL

The KahMahTZ makes the same sound as the PahTahCH and is also written below the line.

Write **KahMahTZ** below the letters

LET'S WRITE WORDS!

אָב

Use the remaining space to write each word several more times.

'ahV
Father

אָב

'ahBah'
Daddy

אַבָּא

Bah'
Comes

בָּא

אָב

אַבָּא

בָּא

אָב

LET'S WRITE IN CURSIVE

Notice that Hebrew Cursive doesn't connect the letters in a word like English Cursive does.

'ahV
Father

'ahBah'
Daddy

Bah'
Comes

THE LETTER "GeeMehL"

The letter GeeMehL looks like a Guy playing Golf. It always makes the sound of the g in golf or guy. It never sounds like the g in giraffe.

λ

"**GeeMehL**" CURSIVE

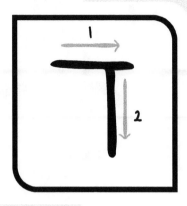

THE LETTER "DahLehT"

The letter DahLehT looks like a
door. It makes the sound of the
English letter "D".

"DahLehT" CURSIVE

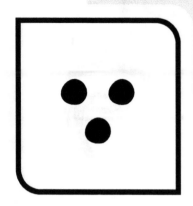

THE "**SehGohL**" VOWEL

The SehGohL makes the sound of the English letter combination "eh" or the "e" in "net" or "bed". The SehGohL hangs below the line.

Write **SehGohL** below the letters

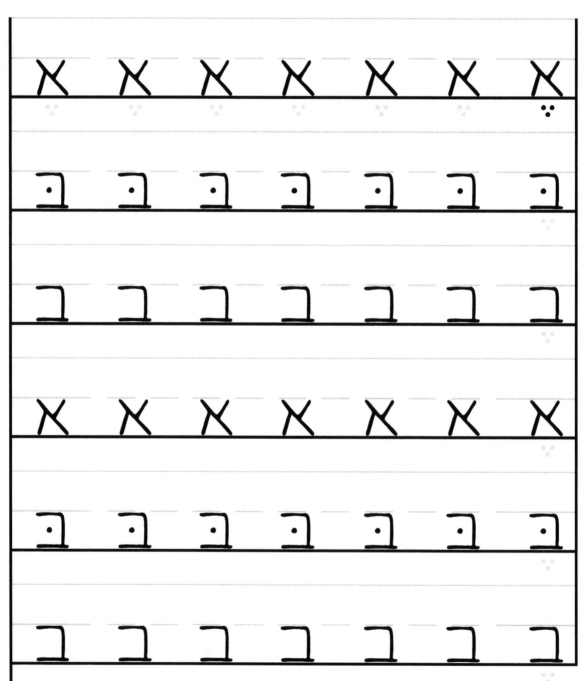

THE "TZehYRehH" VOWEL

The TZehYRehH makes the same sound as SehGohL and just like the SehGohL the TZehYRehH hangs below the line.

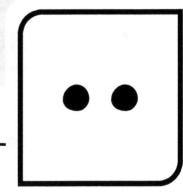

Write **TZehYRehH** below the letters

אָ אָ אָ אָ אָ אָ אָ

בְּ בְּ בְּ בְּ בְּ בְּ בְּ

בֵ בֵ בֵ בֵ בֵ בֵ בֵ

אָ אָ אָ אָ אָ אָ אָ

בְּ בְּ בְּ בְּ בְּ בְּ בְּ

בֵ בֵ בֵ בֵ בֵ בֵ בֵ

LET'S WRITE WORDS!

Use the remaining space to write each word several more times.

DahG
Fish

GehV
Seasonal Pool

GahG
Roof

GahD
Gad (the tribe)

BahD
Cloth

BehGehD
Clothing

'ahGahV
by-the-way

LET'S WRITE IN CURSIVE

DahG
Fish

ﺣﻪﺩ

GehV
Seasonal Pool

ﺩﺣ

GahG
Roof

ﺣﺣ

GahD
Gad (the tribe)

ﺩﺣ

BahD
Cloth

ﺩﻪ

BehGehD
Clothing

ﺩﺣﻪ

'ahGahV
by-the-way

ﺩﺣﺍﻉ

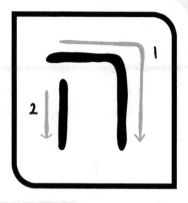

THE LETTER "HehY"

HehY looks like a House with a Hole to let out the smoke. It makes the sound of the English letter "H".

ה

"**HehY**" CURSIVE

ה

THE LETTER "VahV"

The letter VahV looks like a Vanilla bean. It makes the sound of the English letter "V".

"VahV" CURSIVE

THE **"CHohLahM"** VOWEL

The CHohLahM sounds like the English letter combination "oh." Sometimes you'll find just the dot of the CHohLahM floating above and to the left of a letter. It still adds the same "oh" sound.

"CHohLahM" CURSIVE

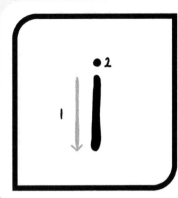

The CHohLahM vowel and the SHooRooK vowel (on the next page) look slightly different in Cursive. The rest of the vowels look exactly the same in Block and Cursive.

THE **"SHooRooK"** VOWEL

The SHooRooK sounds like the English letter combination "oo".

"**SHooRook**" CURSIVE

The SHooRooK vowel and the CHohLahM vowel look slightly different in Cursive. The rest of the vowels look exactly the same in Block and Cursive.

LET'S WRITE WORDS!

וָו

Use the remaining space to write each word several more times.

Hoo'
He

הוּא

DohV
Bear

דוֹב

HehD
Echo

הֵד

HahGahDahH
(Passover)
Hagada

הַגָּדָה

VahV
Hook

וָו

DohDahH
Aunt

דוֹדָה

HehGehH
Steering-
wheel

הֶגֶה

LET'S WRITE IN CURSIVE

דוב

Hoo'
He

הוּא

DohV
Bear

דוֹב

HehD
Echo

הֵד

HahGahDahH
(Passover) Hagada

הַגָּדָה

VahV
Hook

וָו

DohDahH
Aunt

דוֹדָה

HehGehH
Steering-wheel

הֶגֶה

THE LETTER **"ZahYeeN"**

The letter ZahYeeN looks like a Zipper. It makes the sound of the English letter "Z".

"ZahYeeN" CURSIVE

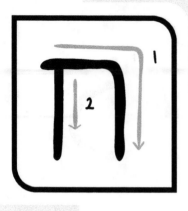

THE LETTER "CHehT"

The letter CHehT looks like a house without a hole. It makes the sound of someone choking, or the CH in Bach.

ח

"CHehT" CURSIVE

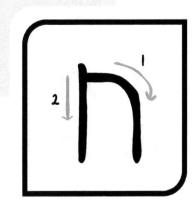

ח

THE LETTER **"TehT"**

The letter TehT has a lovely Tail.
It makes the sound of the English
letter "T".

"TehT" CURSIVE

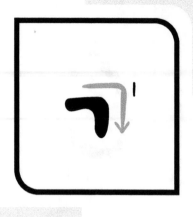

THE LETTER **"YooD"**

The letter Yood looks like a Yawn. It makes the sound of the English letter "Y".

Don't confuse the YooD with the VahV. Although they are similar, the YooD only comes halfway down from the top.

"YooD" CURSIVE

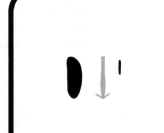

יָד

LET'S WRITE WORDS!

Use the remaining space to write each word several more times.

חג

CHahG
Holiday

זָהָב

ZahHahV
Gold

טוב

TohV
Good

חַוָה

CHahVahH
The original Hebew form of "Eve"

זוּג

ZooG
Couple

יָד

YahD
Hand

יַחַד

YahChahD
Together

LET'S WRITE IN CURSIVE

חַוָּה

חַג	**CHahG** Holiday
לָהָב	**ZahHahV** Gold
טוֹב	**TohV** Good
חַוָּה	**CHahVahH** The original Hebew form of "Eve"
זוּג	**ZooG** Couple
יָד	**YahD** Hand
יַחַד	**YahChahD** Together

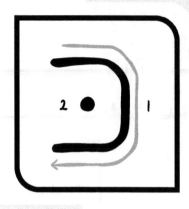

THE LETTER "KahF"

The letter KahF looks like a poor fellow coughing on a candy. It makes the sound of the English letter "K".

Although KahF is similar to BehT, the BehT has sharper corners and a foot that sticks out to the right, while the KahF is completely rounded.

"**KahF**" CURSIVE

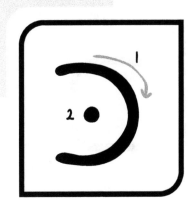

THE LETTER "CHahF"

The letter CHahF is just like the KahF but without the dot. This poor fellow is totally choking. The CHahF makes a chokey sound like the CH in Bach.

"CHahF" CURSIVE

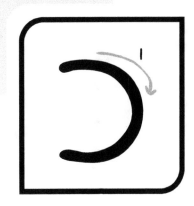

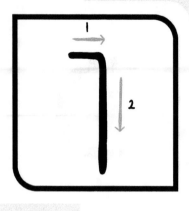

THE "Final CHahF"

If there is a CHahF at the end of a word the bottom part of the CHahF will be stretched down below the line. You will only see this letter at the end of a word.

The Final ChahF is an extra long letter. It descends into the row below the line. When there is a vowel paired with the Final ChahF, the vowel is written slightly **to the left** of the part of the letter that hangs below the line.

"Final CHahF" CURSIVE

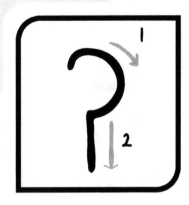

When there is a vowel paired with the Cursive Final CHahF, the vowel is written slightly **to the right** of the part of the letter that hangs below the line.

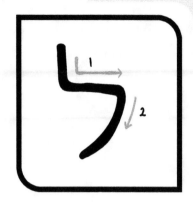

THE LETTER **"LahMehD"**

The letter LahMehD has a Lap.
It makes the sound of the English
letter "L".

The LahMehD is an extra tall letter. It begins in the row above the tops of the other letters.

"LahMehD" CURSIVE

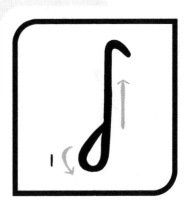

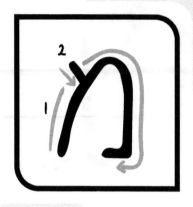

THE LETTER "MehM"

The letter MehM looks like a Mountain with a flag planted just before the peak. It makes the sound of The English letter "M".

מ

"MehM" CURSIVE

N N N N N N N

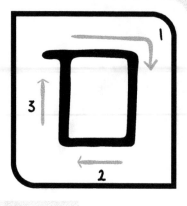

THE **"Final MehM"**

If a MehM is at the end of a word it looks
a little different. You will only see the Final
MehM at the end of a word.

"Final MehM" CURSIVE

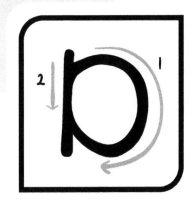

p p p p p p p

GIVE
YOURSELF A
PAT ON THE
BACK :)
YOU'RE
MORE THAN
HALFWAY
THROUGH THE
ALEFBET!

THE "CHeeReeK" VOWEL

The CHeeReeK makes the sound of the English letter combination "ee." It's just one little dot that hangs below the line.

Write **CHeeReeK** below the letters

א א א א א א א א

ב ב ב ב ב ב ב ב

ג ג ג ג ג ג ג ג ג

ד ד ד ד ד ד ד ד

ו ו ו ו ו ו ו ו ו ו

ת ת ת ת ת ת ת

LET'S WRITE WORDS!

כּוֹכָב

Use the remaining space to write each word several more times.

כּוֹכָב

לֹא

מַבּוּל

מַיִם

כָּמוֹךָ

גַּלִּים

אָחִיךָ

KohChahV

Star

Notice the differences between the KahF (has a dot), the ChahF (no dot) and the VehT (has a foot that sticks out to the right.)

Loh'

No

Notice the tall height of the LahMehD.

MahBool

Flood

MahYeeM

Water

Notice how small the YooD is in context with the other letters. It hovers at the height of the other letters.

KahMohCHah

Like you

Notice how the Final ChahF descends into the row below the line and where the vowel is placed.

GahLeeYM

Waves

ahCHeeYCHah

Your brother

מִַים

LET'S WRITE IN CURSIVE

KohChahV

Star

כּוֹכָב

Loh'

No

לֹא

MahBool

Flood

מַבּוּל

MahYeeM

Water

מַיִם

KahMohCHah

Like you

Notice the vowel is placed to the right of the Cursive Final CHahF

כָּמוֹךָ

GahLeeYM

Waves

גַלִּים

ahCHeeYCHah

Your brother

אָחִיךָ

THE LETTER "NooN"

The letter NooN looks like a nose. It makes the sound of the English letter "N".

Don't confuse the NooN with the CHahF. The head and base of the NooN are about half as wide as the head and base of the CHahF.

"**NooN**" CURSIVE

THE **"Final NooN"**

The Final NooN is only found at the end of a word. It looks like the regular NooN with the base pulled down. The letter now stretches below the line.

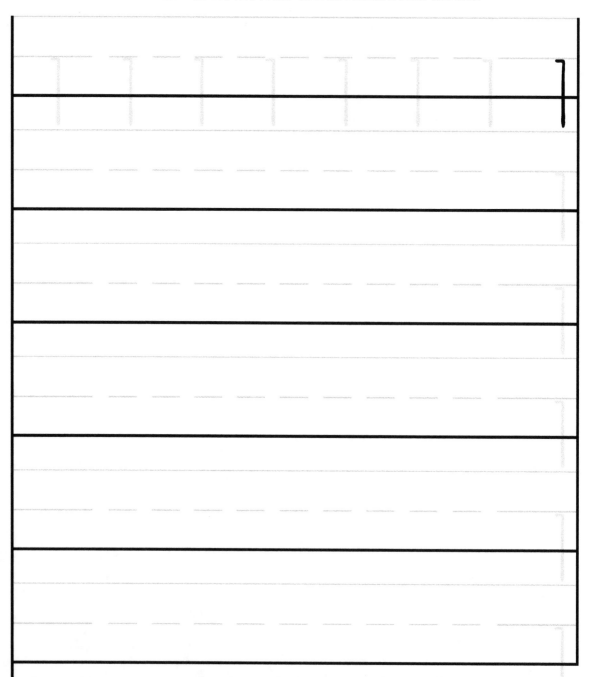

The Final NooN is an extra long letter. The bottom stretches into the row below. Don't confuse the Final NooN with the Final CHahF. The head of the Final NooN is about half as wide as the head of the Final CHahF

"Final NooN" CURSIVE

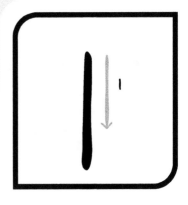

Don't confuse the Cursive Final Noon with the Cursive YooD or the Cursive VahV. The Cursive YooD is smallest, hovering at the height of most of the letters. The Cursive VahV is an average size letter. The Final NooN is long, and descends into the row below.

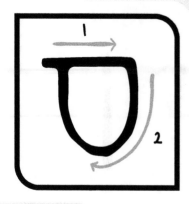

THE LETTER "SahMehCH"

The letter SahMehCH is super circular. It makes the sound of the English letter "S".

Don't confuse the SahMehCH with the Final MehM. The Final MehM has sharper corners while the SahMehCH is circular.

"SahMehCH" CURSIVE

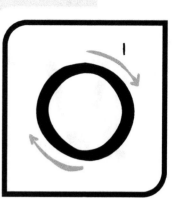

THE LETTER " 'ahYeeN "

The letter 'ahYeeN is silent. He's
silently reading a book.

" 'ahYeeN " CURSIVE

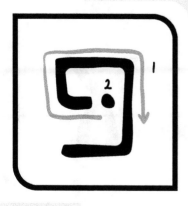

THE LETTER "PehH"

The letter PehH looks like a face with a pimple. It makes the sound of the English letter "P".

"PehH" CURSIVE

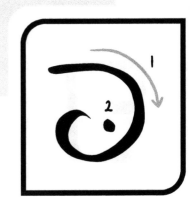

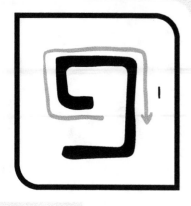

THE LETTER **"FehH"**

The letter FehH looks like a face. It makes the sound of the English letter "F".

"FehH" CURSIVE

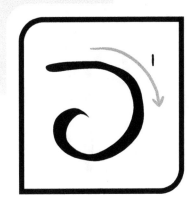

THE "Final FehH"

The Final FehH is only found at the end of a word. It looks just like the FehH but the bottom of the letter is pulled down below the line.

"Final FehH" CURSIVE

BREAK FOR CAKE :)
YOU'RE DOING GREAT!

THE "**SH-Vah**" VOWEL

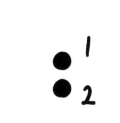

This vowel halts the flow of the word as a hyphen does in a hyphenated word like up-to-date. Sometimes you'll find the SH-Vah together with another vowel. When this happens ignore the SH-Vah.

Write **SH-Vah** below the letters

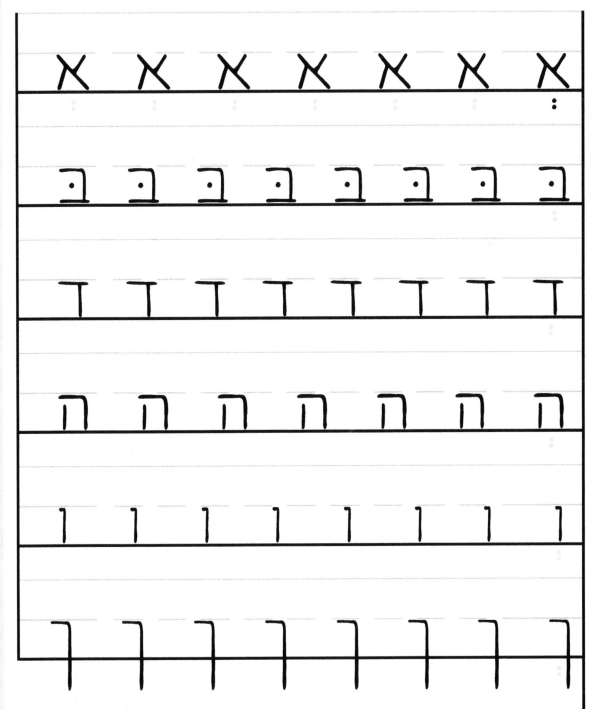

LET'S WRITE WORDS!

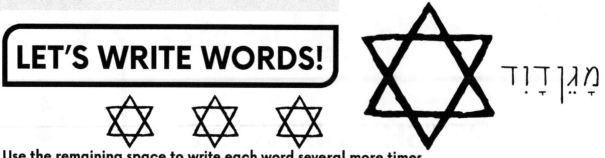

מָגֵן דָּוִד

Use the remaining space to write each word several more times.

YahFehH
Nice

יָפֶה יָפֶה יָפֶה יָפֶה

'ehZ-RahH
Help

עֶזְרָה

NahVeeY'
Prophet

נָבִיא

YahM SooF
Sea of Reeds
(Red Sea)

יַם סוּף

GahN 'ehDehN
Garden
of Eden

גַּן עֵדֶן

P-SeeYahH
Step/Stride

פְּסִיעָה

MahGehN DahVeeD
Shield of David
(Star of David)

מָגֵן דָּוִד

78

LET'S WRITE IN CURSIVE

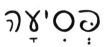

פְּסִיעָה

YahFehH Nice	יָפֶה
'ehZ-RahH Help	עֶזְרָה
NahVeeY' Prophet	נָבִיא
YahM SooF Sea of Reeds (Red Sea)	יַם סוּף
GahN 'ehDehN Garden of Eden	גַּן עֵדֶן
P-SeeYahH Step/Stride	פְּסִיעָה
MahGehN DahVeeD Shield of David (Star of David)	מָגֵן דָּוִד

THE LETTER **"TZahDeeK"**

The TZahDeeK makes a TZ sound. It's pronounced like the English letter combination T and S like in Pat's Place, or the two Z's in pizza.

Don't confuse the TZahDeeK with the 'ahYeeN.

"TZahDeeK" CURSIVE

3

3 3 3 3 3 3 3

3

3

3

3

3

THE "Final TZahDeeK"

The Final TZahDeeK is only found at the end of a word.

"Final TZahDeeK" CURSIVE

Don't confuse the Cursive Final TZahDeeK with the Cursive Final FehH. The difference is in the final tip of the letter. The Cursive Final TZahDeeK finishes with a tip turning upwards. The Cursive Final FehH finishes with a tip turning downwards.

THE LETTER "KooF"

The letter KooF looks like a key.
It sounds like the English letter K.

"KooF" CURSIVE

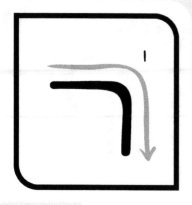

THE LETTER **"RehSH"**

The letter RehSH looks like a
Rainbow. It makes the sound of the
English letter R.

Don't confuse the RehSH with the DahLehT. The RehSH has a rounded shoulder
while the DahLehT has a sharp corner with an extension that sticks out the right
of the letter.

"**RehSH**" CURSIVE

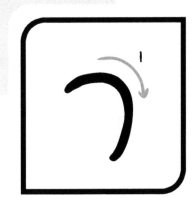

THE "KooBooTZ" VOWEL

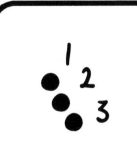

The KooBooTZ looks like three diagonal dots hanging below the line. It makes the sound of the English letter combination "oo".

Write **KooBooTZ** below the letters

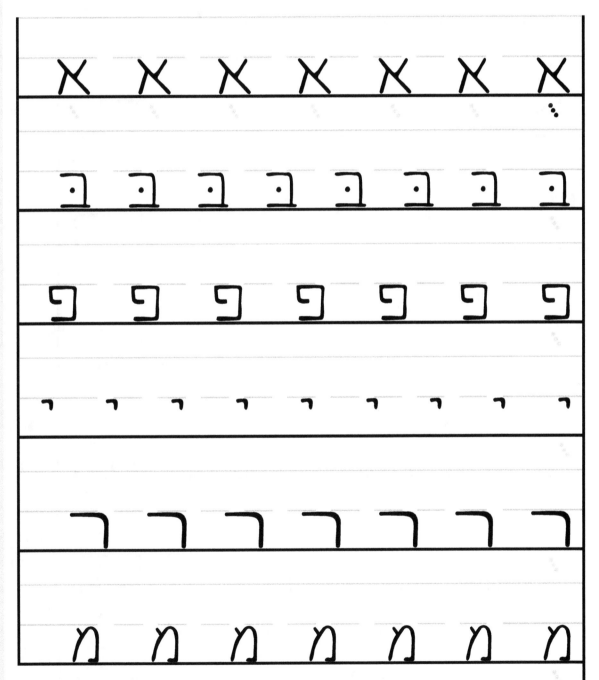

LET'S WRITE WORDS!

קֻפָּה

Use the remaining space to write each word several more times.

צַדִּיק	**TZahDeeYK** Righteous
צֵל	**TZehL** Shadow/Shade
רוֹפֵא	**RohFeh'** Doctor
קֻפָּה	**KooPahH** Money Box
חָמוּץ	**CHahMooTZ** Sour
קָפֶה	**KahFehH** Coffee
רָץ	**RahTZ** Running

LET'S WRITE IN CURSIVE

קָפֶה

TZahDeeYK Righteous	צַדִּיק
TZehL Shadow/Shade	צֵל
RohFeh' Doctor	רוֹפֵא
KooPahH Money Box	קֻפָּה
CHahMooTZ Sour	חָמוּץ
KahFehH Coffee	קָפֶה
RahTZ Running	רָץ

THE LETTER "SHeeN"

The letter SHeeN has a dot on the top right. It makes the sound of the English letter combination "SH".

"SHeeN" CURSIVE

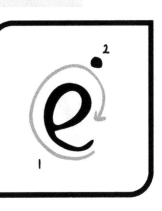

THE LETTER "SeeN"

The letter SeeN has a dot on the top left. You can tell the SHeeN and SeeN apart by remembering this little sentence : "If its not right it's a sin(SeeN)". The SeeN makes the sounds of the English letter "S".

"SeeN" CURSIVE

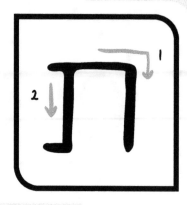

THE LETTER **"TahF"**

The letter TahF has a toe sticking out. It makes the sound of the English letter "T".

ת

Don't confuse the TahF with the CHehT. The TahF has a "toe" that sticks out to the left of the letter.

"TahF" CURSIVE

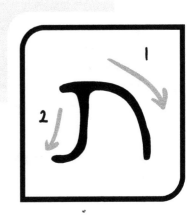

LET'S WRITE WORDS!

שָׂדֶה

Use the remaining space to write each word several more times.

אֱמֶת	**'ehMehT** Truth
שֵׁם	**SHehM** Name
שַׁבָּת	**SHahBahT** Saturday, Sabbath
קָדוֹשׁ	**KahDohSH** Holy
תּוֹרָה	**TohRahH** Torah
שָׂדֶה	**SahDehH** Field
יִשְׂרָאֵל	**YeeS-Rah'-ehL** Israel

אֱמֶת	**'ehMehT** Truth
שֵׁם	**SHehM** Name
שַׁבָּת	**SHahBahT** Saturday
קָדוֹשׁ	**KahDohSH** Holy
תּוֹרָה	**TohRahH** Torah
שָׂדֶה	**SahDehH** Field
יִשְׂרָאֵל	**YeeS-Rah'-ehL** Israel

HOORAY!

YOU CAN NOW WRITE ALL THE LETTERS IN THE ALEFBET. LET'S PRACTICE WRITING SOME COMMON VOCABULARY WORDS.

KehN
Yes

כֵּן

Loh'
No

לֹא

GahDohL
Big

גָּדוֹל

TohV
Good

טוֹב

SHahLohM
Peace.
Used like "hello"

שָׁלוֹם

MahH SH-LohM-CHah?
How are you?(M)

מֶה שְׁלוֹמְךָ?

MahH SH-LohMehCH
How are you?(F)

מֶה שְׁלוֹמֵךְ?

'ahNeeY B-SehDehR
I'm fine

אֲנִי בְּסֵדֶר

BahRooCH HahSHehM
Bless G-d.
Used like "Thank G-d"

בָּרוּךְ הַשֵּׁם

BohKehR TohV
Good morning

בֹּקֶר טוֹב

'ehRehV TohV
Good evening

עֶרֶב טוֹב

LahY-LahH TohV
Good night

לַיְלָה טוֹב

TohDahH
Thank you

תּוֹדָה

TohDahH RahBahH
Thanks a lot

תּוֹדָה רַבָּה

MahH NeeSH-Mah'?
How are you?

מָה נִשְׁמָע?

MahH KohRehH?
What's happening?

מָה קוֹרֶה?

L-HeeT-Rah'ohT
See you soon

לְהִתְרָאוֹת

B-VahKahSHahH
Please

בְּבַקָשָׁה

B-'ehZ-RahT HahSHehM
With G-d's help.
Used like "G-d willing" or "hopefully."

בְּעֶזְרַת הַשֵׁם

S-LeeYCHahH
Excuse me/Sorry

סְלִיחָה

Nah'eeYM M-'ohD
Very nice.
Used like "very nice to meet you"

נָעִים מְאוֹד

LahB-ReeYooT
To health.
Used like "bless you" when
someone sneezes.

לִבְרִיאוּת

'ehYCH KohR-' eeYM L-CHah?
How are you called?
Used like "what's you name?"(M)

אֵיךְ קוֹרְאִים לְךָ?

'ehYCH KohR-' eeYM LahCH?
How are you called?
Used like "what's you name?"(F)

אֵיךְ קוֹרְאִים לָךְ?

Meh'ehYFoh 'ahTahH
Where are you from?(M)

מֵאֵיפֹה אַתָּה?

Meh'ehYFoh 'ahT
Where are you from?(F)

מֵאֵיפֹה אַתְּ?

'ahNeeY
I or Me

אֲנִי

Meh'ahR-TZohT HahB-ReeYT
From the United States

מֵאַרְצוֹת הַבְּרִית

'ehYFohH 'ahTahH GahR
Where do you live?(M)

אֵיפֹה אַתָּה גָּר?

'ehYFohH 'ahT GahRahH
Where do you live?(F)

אֵיפֹה אַתְּ גָּרָה?

'ahNeeY GahR
I live(M)

אֲנִי גָּר

'ahNeeY GahRahH
I live(F)

אֲנִי גָּרָה

BeeYRooSHahLahYeeM
In Jerusalem

בִּירוּשָׁלַיִם

MahH
What?

מָה?

MeeY ZehH
Who's this?

מִי זֶה?

KahR LeeY
I'm cold

קַר לִי

CHahM LeeY
I'm hot

חַם לִי

MahH HahK-TohVehT
What's the address?

מַה הַכְּתֹבֶת?

GahDohL
Big

גָדוֹל

KahTahN
Small

קָטָן

KahMahH ZehH 'ohLehH
How much does this cost?

כַּמָּה זֶה עוֹלֶה?

MahTahY
When?

מָתַי?

'ehYFohH
Where?

אֵיפֹה?

HahKohL B-SehDehR
Everything's fine

הַכֹּל בְּסֵדֶר

PahToo-ahCH
Open

פָּתוּחַ

SahGooR
Closed

סָגוּר

'ahNeeY RohTZehH
I want...(M)

אֲנִי רוֹצֶה

'ahNeeY RohTZahH
I want...(F)

אֲנִי רוֹצָה

'ahNeeY M-CHahPehS
I'm looking for...(M)

אֲנִי מְחַפֵּשׂ

'ahNeeY M-ChahPehSehT
I'm looking for...(F)

אֲנִי מְחַפֶּשֶׂת

S-LeeYCHahH
Excuse me/Sorry

סְלִיחָה

**GREAT JOB!
NOW LET'S
PRACTICE THE
VOCABULARY
WORDS IN
CURSIVE!**

KehN
Yes

ᒉ

Loh'
No

ᒉ·ᑕ

GahDohL
Big

ᑐᒉᓵᒉ

TohV
Good

ᒉᓵᒉ

SHahLohM
Peace.
Used like "hello"

שָׁלוֹם

MahH SH-LohM-CHah?
How are you?(M)

מַה שְׁלוֹמְךָ?

MahH SH-LohMehCH
How are you?(F)

מַה שְׁלוֹמֵךְ?

'ahNeeY B-SehDehR
I'm fine

אֲנִי בְּסֵדֶר

BahRooCH HahSHehM
Bless G-d.
Used like "Thank G-d"

בָּרוּךְ הַשֵּׁם

BohKehR TohV
Good morning

בּוֹקֶר טוֹב

'ehRehV TohV
Good evening

עֶרֶב טוֹב

LahY-LahH TohV
Good night

לַיְלָה טוֹב

TohDahH
Thank you

תּוֹדָה

TohDahH RahBahH
Thanks a lot

תּוֹדָה רַבָּה

MahH NeeSH-Mah'?
How are you?

מָה נִשְׁמָע?

MahH KohRehH?
What's happening?

מָה קוֹרֶה?

L-HeeT-Rah'ohT
See you later

לְהִתְרָאוֹת

B-VahKahSHahH
Please

בְּבַקָשָׁה

B-'ehZ-RahT HahSHehM
With G-d's help. Used like
G-d willing or hopefully

בְּעֶזְרַת הַשֵׁם

S-LeeYCHahH
Excuse me/Sorry

סְלִיחָה

Nah'eeYM M-'ohD
Very nice.
Used like "very nice to meet you."

נָעִים מְאוֹד

LahB-ReeYooT
To health.
Used like "bless you" when
someone sneezes

לַבְּרִיוּת

'ehYCH KohR-' eeYM L-CHah?
How are you called?
Used like "what's your name?"(M)

אֵיךְ קוֹרְאִים לְךָ?

'ehYCH KohR-' eeYM LahCH?
How are you called?
Used like "what's your name?"(F)

אֵיךְ קוֹרְאִים לָךְ?

Meh'ehYFoh 'ahTahH
Where are you from?(M)

מֵאֵיפֹה אַתָּה?

Meh'ehYFoh 'ahT
Where are you from?(F)

מֵאֵיפֹה אַתְּ?

'ahNeeY
I or Me

אֲנִי

Meh'ahR-TZohT HahB-ReeYT
From the United States

מֵאַרְצוֹת הַבְּרִית

'ehYFohH 'ahTahH GahR
Where do you live?(M)

אֵיפֹה אַתָּה גָּר?

'ehYFohH 'ahT GahRahH
Where do you live?(F)

אֵיפֹה אַתְּ גָּרָה?

'ahNeeY GahR
I live(M)

אֲנִי גָּר

'ahNeeY GahRahH
I live(F)

אֲנִי גָּרָה

BeeYRooSHahLahYeeM
In Jerusalem

בִּירוּשָׁלַיִם

MahH
What?

מָה?

MeeY ZehH
Who's this?

מִי זֶה?

KahR LeeY
I'm cold

קַר לִי

124

CHahM LeeY
I'm hot

חַם לִי

MahH HahK-TohVehT
What's the address?

מָה הַכְּתֹבֶת?

GahDohL
Big

גָּדוֹל

KahTahN
Small

קָטָן

KahMahH ZehH 'ohLehH
How much does this cost?

כַּמָּה זֶה עוֹלֶה?

MahTahY
When?

מָתַי?

'ehYFohH
Where?

אֵיפֹה?

HahKohL B-SehDehR
Everything's fine

הַכֹּל בְּסֵדֶר

PahToo-ahCH
Open

פָּתוּחַ

SahGooR
Closed

סָגוּר

'ahNeeY RohTZehH
I want...(M)

אֲנִי רוֹצֶה

'ahNeeY RohTZahH
I want...(F)

אֲנִי רוֹצָה

'ahNeeY M-CHahPehS
I'm looking for...(M)

אֲנִי מְחַפֵּשׂ

'ahNeeY M-ChahPehSehT
I'm looking for...(F)

אֲנִי מְחַפֶּשֶׂת

S-LeeYCHahH
Excuse me/Sorry

סְלִיחָה

LET'S CELEBRATE!

You did it! You've accomplished the next big step to Hebrew fluency. You now have the tools to write any Hebrew word. Before long, you'll be able to write as smoothly and as easily as you do in English. Learning new skills is so valuable to the human mind. Especially new languages that broaden your mind. So much more so Hebrew which has the added potential to broaden your spiritual perspective.

I'm so happy you chose to spend your time, effort and energy learning to write Hebrew with me. Thank you! And congratulations on your new and beautiful life skill! **YOU can write in Hebrew!**

ABOUT THE AUTHOR

Miiko is the author of the best selling book *Learn to Read Hebrew in 6 Weeks!* Her unique method of teaching Hebrew Reading has taught tens of thousands of people around the world to read Hebrew. It is currently available in English and Spanish and is in the process of being translated to Arabic.

Miiko lives in Be'er Sheva, Israel with her husband Aaron and their nine kids. She loves hosting Shabbat meals, exploring Israel and teaching Pilates.

Printed in the USA
CPSIA information can be obtained
at www.ICGtesting.com
LVHW060235040823
754333LV00019B/1370

9 780997 867558